T3-BEA-052

Language Arts Grade 3

TABLE OF CONTENTS

Page Number(s)

GRAMMAR & SENTENCES

Language Arts Grade 3
Grammar & Sentences

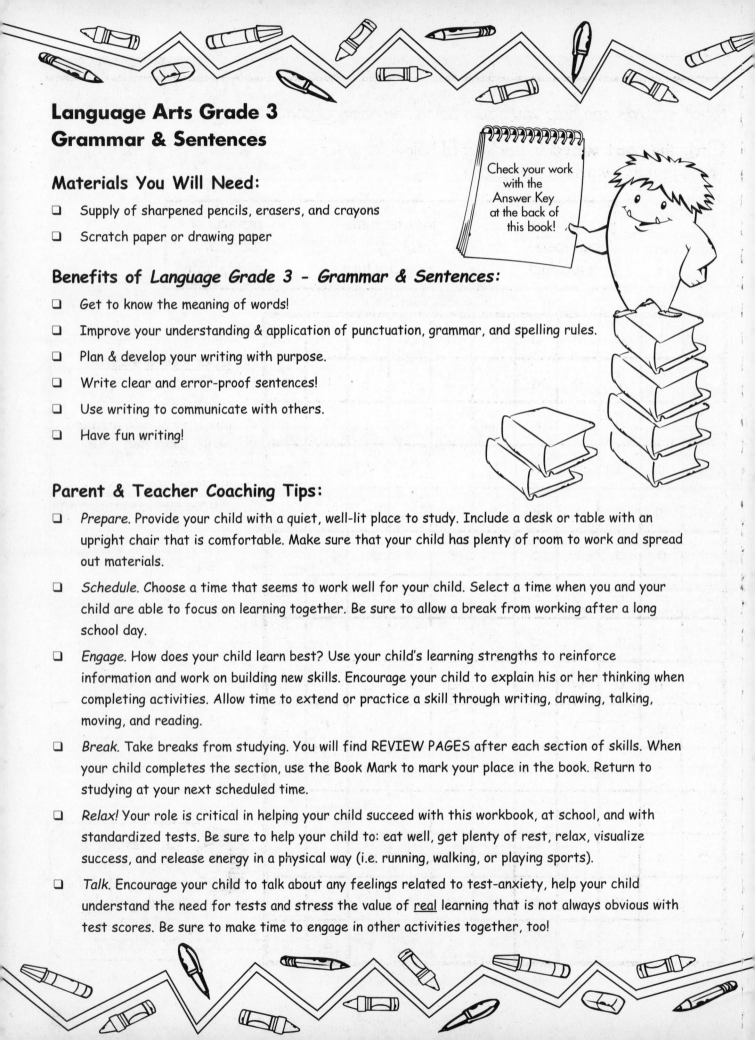

Materials You Will Need:

❑ Supply of sharpened pencils, erasers, and crayons

❑ Scratch paper or drawing paper

Check your work with the Answer Key at the back of this book!

Benefits of *Language Grade 3 - Grammar & Sentences*:

❑ Get to know the meaning of words!

❑ Improve your understanding & application of punctuation, grammar, and spelling rules.

❑ Plan & develop your writing with purpose.

❑ Write clear and error-proof sentences!

❑ Use writing to communicate with others.

❑ Have fun writing!

Parent & Teacher Coaching Tips:

❑ *Prepare.* Provide your child with a quiet, well-lit place to study. Include a desk or table with an upright chair that is comfortable. Make sure that your child has plenty of room to work and spread out materials.

❑ *Schedule.* Choose a time that seems to work well for your child. Select a time when you and your child are able to focus on learning together. Be sure to allow a break from working after a long school day.

❑ *Engage.* How does your child learn best? Use your child's learning strengths to reinforce information and work on building new skills. Encourage your child to explain his or her thinking when completing activities. Allow time to extend or practice a skill through writing, drawing, talking, moving, and reading.

❑ *Break.* Take breaks from studying. You will find REVIEW PAGES after each section of skills. When your child completes the section, use the Book Mark to mark your place in the book. Return to studying at your next scheduled time.

❑ *Relax!* Your role is critical in helping your child succeed with this workbook, at school, and with standardized tests. Be sure to help your child to: eat well, get plenty of rest, relax, visualize success, and release energy in a physical way (i.e. running, walking, or playing sports).

❑ *Talk.* Encourage your child to talk about any feelings related to test-anxiety, help your child understand the need for tests and stress the value of <u>real</u> learning that is not always obvious with test scores. Be sure to make time to engage in other activities together, too!

Name:_____   Date:_____

Root words can help you figure out the meaning of some words.

Circle the **root word** in each word below.
Then, find the words in the puzzle.

aquarium	thermometer	podiatrist
centipede	geology	manual
aquaduct	manufacture	geography

a	t	b	n	u	k	h	d	s	a	e
r	h	r	a	q	u	a	r	i	u	m
t	e	q	x	o	i	t	y	p	l	a
l	r	z	a	n	b	c	v	e	o	n
e	m	g	j	k	e	t	p	u	s	u
p	o	d	i	a	t	r	i	s	t	f
o	m	o	o	q	r	t	a	m	n	a
p	e	m	v	o	d	s	x	u	i	c
w	t	a	w	e	r	g	v	g	l	t
c	e	n	t	i	p	e	d	e	t	u
x	r	u	n	l	z	m	o	o	s	r
v	n	a	r	r	q	o	u	l	v	e
b	o	l	s	c	a	o	e	o	m	r
a	q	u	a	d	u	c	t	g	k	a
g	e	o	g	r	a	p	h	y	c	p

Root Word Bank

aqua – water
man – hand
metri/meter – to measure
ped(e)/pod/ped – foot
geo – earth
therm – heat

Challenge: Do you know the meaning of all the words in the box? Look them up in the dictionary!

Write your own new words from each **root word** below.

1. dent (tooth) _____

2. magn (large) _____

3. min (small) _____

4. super (over/above) _____

5. poly (many/several) _____

6. script (to write) _____

7. hydro (water) _____

8. ann or enni (year) _____

Choose one of the words that you wrote above. Look it up in the dictionary and write the definition. Then, draw a picture to illustrate your word.

_____

_____

_____

We can create a new word by adding a **prefix** to the beginning of a word.

prefix   +   root word   =   new word

mal   +   nutrition   =   **mal**nutrition

prefix	meaning
mal-	bad
pre-	before
inter-	between
ambi-	both
anti-	against
dis-	apart or not
micro-	small
poly-	many
sub-	under

Add a **prefix** from the box to make a new word.

	prefix	word	new word with **prefix**
1.	_____	state	_____
2.	_____	marine	_____
3.	_____	function	_____
4.	_____	view	_____
5.	_____	dexterous	_____
6.	_____	standard	_____
7.	_____	engage	_____
8.	_____	social	_____
9.	_____	scope	_____
10.	_____	unsaturated	_____

Tip:
Use a dictionary or the
prefix and meaning box if
you need help.

Prefixes can help you identify the meaning of new words.

prefix	meaning
sub-	under or below
non-	not or no
semi-	half or part
inter-	between

Look at the words, the **prefixes**, and the definitions. Match each word to the correct definition. Write the letter that best represents the definition for each word.

1. _____ subzero

2. _____ subway

3. _____ non-existent

4. _____ intercontinental

5. _____ substandard

6. _____ nonsense

7. _____ submerge

8. _____ international

9. _____ intermission

10. _____ interoffice

11. _____ semicircle

12. _____ interchange

13. _____ non-stop

14. _____ semiformal

15. _____ semipro

A. Making no sense

B. Below standard

C. To place under water

D. Between offices

E. Traveling between continents

F. Underground transportation

G. Between acts of a play or performance

H. Half of a circle

I. Below freezing

J. Part formal and part casual

K. Half-way to becoming a professional

L. Not real or present

M. Continuing with no stops

N. Between countries or nations

O. Exchanging things between two people

Name:_____ Date:_____

We can create a new word by adding a **suffix** to the end of a word.

base word + **suffix** = **new word**
bake   **-er**   bak**er**

suffix	meaning
-er	a person who does something
-est	most
-ful or full	full of
-less	without or lacking

Add the **suffix -er**, **-est**, **-ful**, or **-less** to each **base word** to make a new word.

Base Word   **New Word**

1. help _____

2. produce _____

3. smart _____

4. hope _____

5. play _____

6. thought _____

7. manage _____

8. peace _____

9. care _____

10. great _____

11. buy _____

12. drive _____

13. waste _____

14. fish _____

15. harm _____

Suffixes can help you identify
the meaning of new words.

suffix	meaning
-able	capable of or can do
-ery	a place for doing something
-ish	resembling or like
-ous	having a lot of something

Look at the words, the **suffixes**, and the definitions. Match each word to the correct definition. Write the letter that best represents the definition for each word.

1. _____ bakery

2. _____ foolish

3. _____ glamorous

4. _____ readable

5. _____ nursery

6. _____ joyous

7. _____ elfish

8. _____ teachable

9. _____ adventurous

10. _____ spacious

F. A place for baking

C. Resembling a fool

J. Having a lot of glamour

H. Something that you are able to read

D. A place for taking care of plants or children

E. Having a lot of joy & happiness

G. Looking like an elf

A. Capable of being taught

I. Having a great sense of adventure

B. Having a lot of space

Choose one of the words and draw a picture to illustrate it on another sheet of paper. Use the new word in a sentence or two to describe your drawing.

_____

_____

_____

_____

Words that are made up of two smaller words are called **compound words**.

dog   +   house   =   **doghouse**

Write a **compound word** by putting each pair of words together.

1. home + work = _____

2. some + one = _____

3. sun + shine = _____

4. grand + parents = _____

5. night + light = _____

6. sun + set = _____

7. in + side = _____

8. cook + book = _____

9. birth + day = _____

10. play + ground = _____

11. sea + shell = _____

12. sail + boat = _____

13. pan + cake = _____

14. grape + fruit = _____

15. cow + boy = _____

Challenge: On a separate sheet of paper, have a race with a friend to see who can write the most **compound words** in 1 minute. GO!

Tip:
If you can take a word apart and have two separate words, it's a **compound word!**

Make a **compound word** by joining two words together. Add a word from the box to each word below and write it on the line. Then, find each new **compound word** in the puzzle.

1. cup _____

2. pop _____

3. finger _____

4. sun _____

5. foot _____

6. motor _____

7. hot _____

8. data _____

9. class _____

10. news _____

nail

paper

base

cake

glasses

cycle

corn

room

ball

dog

f	o	o	t	b	a	l	l	o	l	p	c	a
i	d	e	c	r	d	h	o	t	d	o	r	t
n	a	s	u	n	g	l	a	s	s	e	s	j
g	t	f	p	o	p	c	o	r	n	l	h	s
e	a	g	c	f	o	h	i	k	b	m	o	e
r	b	q	a	b	l	z	c	x	e	e	t	o
n	a	w	k	v	n	y	d	r	n	m	d	p
a	s	s	e	c	l	a	s	s	r	o	o	m
i	e	o	a	c	t	y	p	l	o	k	g	o
l	m	o	t	o	r	c	y	c	l	e	m	e
l	p	s	n	e	w	s	p	a	p	e	r	q

Name:_____ Date:_____

The word contract means to make smaller. A **contraction** is a word made up of two words that are put together and made into a shorter word.
An **apostrophe** takes the place of the letters that are taken out of the word.

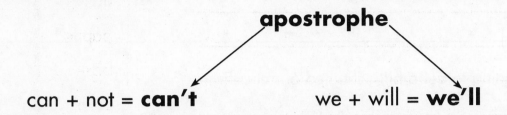

apostrophe

can + not = **can't**   we + will = **we'll**

Use the two words to make a **contraction**.

First word	Second word	Contraction
1. we	are	we're
2. they	are	_____
3. she	is	_____
4. he	is	_____
5. I	am	_____
6. we	have	_____
7. they	have	_____
8. I	have	_____
9. she	has	_____
10. he	has	_____
11. can	not	_____
12. should	not	_____
13. would	not	_____
14. could	not	_____
15. will	not	_____
16. it	is	_____

Challenge:
List as many **contractions** as you can in 3 minutes. Then, write the two words that make each **contraction**.

Read each sentence carefully and circle the correct **contraction** to complete it. Then, rewrite the sentence on the line.

1. (They're, They'll) going to the museum tomorrow.

   _____

2. "(You'd, You're) going to get a hit!" shouted our coach.

   _____

3. I wonder if (it's, isn't) possible to see a double rainbow again.

   _____

4. "(Where's, Where'll) your notebook?" asked my mom.

   _____

5. Andy wondered if (he's, it's) going to rain on Saturday.

   _____

6. The new neighbors wondered if (they're, they've) going to like it here.

   _____

7. They said they have a son and (he's, he'd) just have to get used to it.

   _____

8. Brian wished a cute girl his age had moved in, but (they're, he's) sure the boy will be nice.

   _____

9. Once the neighbors get settled in, (he'll, she's) go visit.

   _____

10. "(You're, Your) going to like their dog, too," said mom.

   _____

An **abbreviation** is a short way to write a word. **Abbreviations** of proper nouns (i.e. names, titles, days of the week, months, and street names) begin with a capital letter and end with a period.

Circle the correct **abbreviation** for each word.

1. August   Aug   Aug.   Ave.
2. Sunday   sun   Sat.   Sun.
3. Street   St.   st.   Sept.
4. Doctor   doc   Dr.   dr.
5. Tuesday   Tues.   T.   Thurs.

Write the correct word for each **abbreviation**.

6. Oct. _____

7. Wed. _____

8. Ave. _____

9. Feb. _____

10. Dec. _____

Rewrite the following sentences with **abbreviations** for the underlined words.

11. On <u>Friday</u>, I went to Sara's house after my appointment with <u>Doctor</u> Smith.

_____

12. She lives on Green <u>Street</u> near Grant <u>Avenue</u>.

_____

13. We were going skating on <u>Saturday</u> and to a movie on <u>Sunday</u>.

_____

14. I haven't seen her since <u>September</u>.

_____

15. It is already <u>November</u>, so we were due for a visit!

_____

Name:_____   Date:_____

Review: Prefixes & Suffixes

Add a **prefix** or **suffix** to complete each word in the sentences.

1. I went to the gas station to _____fill my gas tank.

prefixes	suffixes
un-	-er
re-	-est
pre-	-ful
	-less

2. After I put lotion on my hands they were much soft_____.

3. When you say thank you, you are showing people that you are respect_____.

4. The frown on his face told us that he was _____happy.

5. We took a _____test to see how much we knew before we started the chapter.

6. When you are still and not moving, you are motion_____.

7. One of the great_____ feelings is when someone shows they care about you.

8. She has good foot skills, which makes her an excellent soccer play_____.

Write a sentence using each word.

9. wonderful

_____

10. remake

_____

11. taller

_____

12. unsure

_____

Name:_____   Date:_____

Review: Compound Words, Contractions & Abbreviations

Circle all the **compound words**, underline the **abbreviations**, and draw a box around the **contractions** in the paragraphs below.

Noises in the Night

It's a dark and stormy night and everyone is sleeping on Market St. Well, that's not entirely true. I've been up since midnight listening to the eerie sounds of something that won't let me rest. You're probably wondering what's going on. Let me give you some background.

Dr. and Mrs. Ford lived on the corner of Grant Ave. and Market St., which is just next to Pirate's Pond and the home of a long time legend. The legend has it, that over one hundred years ago, some outlaw pirates took over a ship called the S.S. Mayfair led by Capt. Frye. A huge storm caused a shipwreck and the pirates buried gold coins near the edge of the pond. Over many years, the land was covered by the pond water and the gold coins were never found.

Dr. and Mrs. Ford used to tell tales of hearing noises in the night, but nobody ever believed them. They were sure that it was Capt. Frye and his crew calling out for help! Dr. Ford retired, and he and his wife moved to Fla. Nobody in this town has heard from them since.

My parents bought the Ford's house in Nov. and we moved here shortly after. Every time there's a thunderstorm, I hear strange noises at night and it makes me wonder about this neighborhood legend. I'm not sure what to believe. Do you think the legend is true?

Use a **comma** to separate words in a **series** of three or more things.

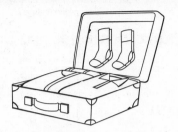

I packed my **shirt, pants, and socks**.

Tip:
Remember to place a **comma** after each word in a series, including the word that is just before "**and**" or "**or**".

Read each sentence. Add **commas** where they belong.

1. We went to the beach and took our sunscreen towels shovels and pails.

2. My mom brought strawberries peaches and watermelon for a healthy snack.

3. We played volleyball tossed the Frisbee and built a sand castle.

4. The days were fun exciting and tiring!

5. When it was time to go, we shook the sand out of our towels blankets and clothes.

6. On the first day of school, I brought my school supplies book bag and lunch box.

7. We talked about fun activities our daily schedule and what we would learn this year.

8. Our teacher told us to read study math facts and share our thoughts about the first day with our family.

9. I can't wait to learn about multiplication division and fractions!

10. I think school is going to be challenging exciting and fun.

Write a sentence about three or more of your favorite foods and snacks. Don't forget the **commas**!

_____

_____

_____

Use a **comma** between the name of a city and state, and between the day and year.

I live in **Columbus, Ohio**.

We moved here on **July 28, 2001**.

Read each sentence. Add **commas** where they belong.

1. For vacation, my family went to Orlando Florida.

2. The last time we were there was March 9 2001.

3. We drove through Memphis Tennessee.

4. Our hotel was just outside of Orlando in Kissimmee Florida.

5. We arrived on December 23 2002.

6. We spent a day at the beach in Orlando Florida.

7. Then we spent a day at my aunt and uncle's house in Tampa Florida.

8. Our family celebrated the New Year on January 1 2003.

9. We checked out of the hotel on January 3 2003.

10. On the way home, we visited our grandparents in Atlanta Georgia.

11. What is the city and state where you live?

_____

12. What day and year were you born?

_____

Every sentence begins with a **capital letter** and ends with a **punctuation mark**.

The party starts at 6:30**.**   A **statement** tells something and ends with a period.

What time is it**?**   A **question** asks something and ends with a question mark.

Let's go**!**   An **exclamation** shows strong feeling and ends with an exclamation point.

Circle the number before the sentences that are written correctly. Rewrite the sentences that are not written correctly.

1. my sister and I went to Lauren's party.

_____

2. We had pizza and it was delicious!

_____

3. Then Lauren opened her presents

_____

4. can you guess what she got

_____

5. lauren's mom gave her a dress.

_____

6. After the gifts were opened, we had cake.

_____

7. the cake was chocolate – my favorite!

_____

8. When we finished our cake, do you know what we played

_____

9. i won a prize for the ring toss game.

_____

10. It was a great party

_____

Name:_____   Date:_____

Remember: A statement ends with a **period**.
A question ends with a **question mark**.
An exclamation ends with an **exclamation point**.

Add a **period**, **question mark**, or **exclamation point** to complete each sentence.

1. Where are you going on vacation _____

2. We are going to New York City _____

3. I have never been there before _____

4. New York City is a great place to visit _____

5. I want to see the Statue of Liberty _____

6. Can we climb to the top and look out _____

7. What else can we do in New York City _____

8. You can go to Central Park or see a show on Broadway _____

9. That sounds like so much fun _____

10. I can't wait _____

11. Write a **statement**.

_____

12. Write a **question**.

_____

13. Write an **exclamation**.

_____

 Challenge: Ask someone to say a **statement**, **question**, or **exclamation**. See if you can tell what kind of sentence it is and what kind of punctuation should come at the end.

Tip: Don't forget to add the correct punctuation!

Cross out each mistake you see in the sentences below. Rewrite each sentence with correct capitalization and punctuation.

1. i cant wait to go to the basketball game tonight?

_____

2. I am excited to be able to go to the championship game.

_____

3. Its girls' night, so I will be going with molly Megan and margaret

_____

4. Do you think I should wear my red blue and gold jersey or my white t-shirt

_____

5. our seats are up really high, but the view is very good!

_____

6. My favorite player really knows how to slam dunk

_____

7. I usually get a snack at the game like peanuts popcorn or a hotdog

_____

8. When I get a large drink I get to keep the souvenir cup

_____

9. Do you know how many fans can fit in the arena

_____

10. who is your favorite player.

_____

11. Last time we went to the game I got a banner a rally towel and a t-shirt

_____

12. do you think our team will score more than 100 points!

_____

Name:_____ Date:_____

Rewrite each **singular noun** below so that it is a **plural noun**, meaning more than one. Then, draw a picture to show one of the **plural nouns**.

1. computer _____

2. cell phone _____

3. party _____

4. radio _____

5. goat _____

6. guinea pig _____

7. fry _____

8. pie _____

9. candy _____

10. daisy _____

11. dish _____

12. fox _____

13. sock _____

14. kiss _____

15. kitty _____

16. city _____

17. page _____

18. pastry _____

19. radish _____

20. tax _____

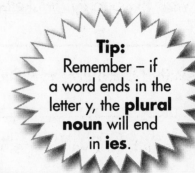

Tip:
Remember – if a word ends in the letter y, the **plural noun** will end in **ies**.

Challenge: Try these **plural word** riddles:
1. What has 4 wheels and flies?
2. What did the frog order at the fast food restaurant?
Check the Answer Key at the back of the book for the answers!

Circle each word that is spelled incorrectly. Rewrite the words correctly on the lines below each sentence.

1. Brenda felt like an uglie duckling becuse she had a pimple on her nose.

   _____   _____

2. It was a beautifull day for flieng kites.

   _____   _____

3. How neately can you write your name backwards without lookiing?

   _____   _____

4. When we enterd the restaurant, the waitress was not that friendley.

   _____   _____

5. We wanteed to order some soft drinks, but the waitress was not being helpfull.

   _____   _____

6. Sarah was hopeing to see the game live, but she was gratefull that it was on TV.

   _____   _____

7. Basketball players are talentid and very powerfull.

   _____   _____

8. Because of the construction, traffic was moveing very slowely.

   _____   _____

9. I had trouble heering my friend's message because she was rambling too quickely.

   _____   _____

10. I climbeed the hill without much difficultey.

   _____   _____

11. Patrick joyned the soccer team late, but he is still playng a lot.

   _____   _____

12. She is certainely welcome to come with you, if she will speak quietely.

   _____   _____

13. We wantedd it to be a surprise, but he was watcheng when we came in with the cake.

   _____   _____

Circle the word in each word pair that is spelled correctly.

1.	abowt	about	beter	better	bring	brieng	carry	carie
2.	clean	cleen	cut	cutt	done	dun	draw	drau
3.	drink	dreenk	aight	eight	fawl	fall	far	farr
4.	fuwl	full	got	gawt	grow	growed	hold	holled
5.	hot	hawt	hurt	hert	iff	if	keap	keep
6.	kind	kined	laff	laugh	light	liegt	longe	long
7.	much	muche	myself	misellf	never	nevr	only	onlee
8.	own	owne	pick	pikk	seven	sehvin	shall	shal
9.	show	shoaw	sicks	six	smowll	small	stahrt	start
10.	tenn	ten	today	todae	togethr	together	trie	try

Choose 3 correctly spelled words from above and use them in a sentence. Draw a picture to go with your sentence.

11. _____

12. _____

13. _____

Challenge: Learn a new word each day. Practice sounding out the words by looking at the letters. Then, practice writing the words. Have a pretend spelling test with your new words.

Name:_____ Date:_____

Read each sentence. Add **commas**, **periods**, **question marks**, or **exclamation marks** where they belong.

1. For my birthday I am having a party with my family friends and neighbors

2. I invited Ian Adam and Eric.

3. Are Robbie Joseph and Noah coming, too

4. What are we having for lunch

5. Yeah I love ice cream

6. What is your favorite kind of ice cream

7. Parties are great

8. Is this present from Mom Dad and Bobby

9. We are having hamburgers cheeseburgers and hotdogs.

10. I love cheeseburgers with ketchup mustard and pickles

11. Dad likes his with lettuce onions and tomatoes, too.

12. We are also having potato salad baked beans and pasta salad.

13. Dessert will be strawberry chocolate and vanilla ice cream

14. We are going to play volleyball have a water balloon toss and go swimming

15. You need to take your time throw carefully and concentrate during the balloon toss.

16. I am looking forward to opening my gifts eating and playing with my friends.

17. Aunt Betty Aunt Rose and Uncle Len each brought a present for me

18. I am really hoping to get a new bike a helmet and a raft for the pool.

19. Family friends and neighbors can have a lot of fun together

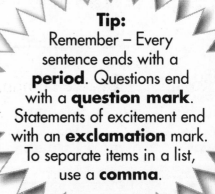

Tip:
Remember – Every sentence ends with a **period**. Questions end with a **question mark**. Statements of excitement end with an **exclamation** mark. To separate items in a list, use a **comma**.

Rewrite each sentence using **capital letters** and the correct **punctuation**.

1. guess what   yesterday we went to the swimming pool

_____

2. jeff ashley and i got really tired from swimming a lot

_____

3. I swam so much i took a nap when we got home

_____

4. What was the best part   the best part was the water slide

_____

5. the line for the twirly twister was long   that's my favorite ride

_____

6. the diving board was exciting, too   it's so high up

_____

7. can ashley dive from the high board   absolutely she is a great diver

_____

8. mom brought healthy snacks for us to eat

_____

9. the snacks helped give us energy so we could ride the super slide

_____

10. i liked the granola bars pretzels and carrot sticks

_____

Name:_____   Date:_____

Review: Punctuation & Spelling

Read each paragraph below. Cross out all **capitalizing** mistakes, **misspelled** words, or incorrect **punctuation**. Above each mistake, write the correct letter, word, or **punctuation** mark. Write in the correct **punctuation** if it is missing.

the giant panda is a fascinating Animal It lives eats and plays in china in the mountains and it uses its special paws to eat bamboo the jiant panda population is geting smaller becuse the panda has been hunted for fur and accidentelly killed in traps set for other animals. The peeple of china have set up areas for pandas to live in safelly. also, it is against the law to hunt the giant panda.

Pizza is my favorite dinner it is a helthy food? one reeson is because it has vegetabels on it. It usualy has crust spices tomato sauce and cheese. It can also hav meet and vegetables like pepperoni sausage and mushrooms. What kind of pizza do you like!

Name:_____   Date:_____

Review: Punctuation & Spelling

Cross out any **misspelled** words, letters that should be **capitalized**, or **punctuation** that is incorrect. Above each mistake, write in the correct word, capital letter, or **punctuation**.

1. making marthas super choclate chip cookies can be a lot of fun

2. reheat the oven grease the cookie sheats and get the ingreedeents.

3. mix shortening brown shugar and white sugar in a bowl until ligt and fluffy.

4. Then add the eggs one at a time and beat them well while stirring in vunilla

5. Mix in the flour baking soda and salt slowly stir until creamy?

6. Finally, fold in the chocolit chips..

7. Now you are ready to drop the cookie doh onto the cookie sheets?

8. Bake the cookies for 8 to 10 minites, or until light broun.

9. When they are dun baking, allow the cookies to cool on the baking sheet

10. then move them to a wire rack to cool completelly

11. enjoy your homemade treets

12. Write two or three correct sentences about *your* favorite cookies!

_____

_____

_____

Name:_____   Date:_____

Review: Punctuation & Spelling

Cross out any **misspelled** words or incorrect **punctuation**. Above the mistakes, write in the correctly **spelled** words and the correct **punctuation**.

1. Reeding is important for many reasons?

2. it helps you to learn new things

3. reading is fun?

4. nathan lieks to read mysterys fiction and action adventures

5. You can pick up a book and take an adventure go on a journey or meet new friends

6. You can reed books like johns day michelles sneezing fit and sheris big win

7. recycling helps make our wurld a healthier and safer place.

8. paul recycles plastic aluminum and paper

9. you can reuse items to make crafts games toys

10. we have a limited amownt of space on Earth,

11. So we shuld recycle as much as we can?

Name:_____ Date:_____

Review: Punctuation & Spelling

Read each paragraph. Cross out all the mistakes you see on each line. Above the mistakes, write in the correctly **spelled** words, **capital letters**, or correct **punctuation**.

Have you ever wondered about flying insects butterfiels and moths. Did you know that there is three mane differences betwean butterflys and mothes. First. butterflys is usually brightlly colored with yellow oringe red and blue Moths are usually dull in color? second, butterflies are active during the day moths are active at night. Third! butterflies form a chrysalis and moths form a cocoon.

do you want to learn how to be a grate cook! For an appetizer, you can makes stuffd mushrooms cheese and crackers or onyin rings? If you like chiken, you may want to makes chicken soup chicken dumplings or chicken parmesan If you prefer vegetarian dishs, you can leanr how to make stir-frie with snow peas carrits and cabbige. For desert you might try chocolate pudding fresh bred with jelly or froot salid. enjoy your yummy treets

STOP! TAKE A BREAK! You did a great job! Place your Book Mark here & RELAX!

A **common noun** names a non-specific person, place, or thing.

person
the gardener

place
the garden

thing
watering can

Circle the **common nouns** in each sentence.

1. The gardener planted his vegetable garden last weekend.

2. The garden is filled with lettuce and tomatoes.

3. Broccoli and carrots are growing too.

4. The gardener waters his garden every day.

5. My mother asked him for some tomatoes.

6. The bunnies in the neighborhood like the carrots.

7. He put up a fence to keep the bunnies out.

8. One bunny squeezed under the fence.

9. The bunny ate two carrots.

10. The gardener chased the bunny out of his garden.

Challenge: Read a favorite story or chapter in a book. On another sheet of paper, make a chart with three sections: person, place, and thing. How many **common nouns** can you find? Write them on the chart under the correct heading.

A **proper noun** names a specific person, place, or thing. **Proper nouns** always begin with a capital letter.

Mr. Green

Circle all the **proper nouns** in each sentence.

1. Where does Grandma Shirley live?

2. She lives in Pittsburgh, Pennsylvania.

3. Her house is on Oak Street.

4. Every year the Wilson family goes to Florida.

5. They have lots of fun swimming in the Atlantic Ocean.

6. David turns ten this year.

7. His birthday is in July.

8. David wants to go to Midtown Bowling Lanes for his birthday.

Think of a specific **proper noun** for each common noun. Write it on the line.

9. a person _____

10. a city _____

11. a movie _____

12. a book _____

13. a teacher _____

14. a month _____

15. a team _____

16. a game _____

17. a store _____

18. a restaurant _____

Name:_____ Date:_____

A noun that names more than one person, place, or thing is called a **plural noun**.

There are four different ways to make a **plural noun**.

1. For most nouns, add **s**	
hat	hat**s**

2. For nouns that end in **x**, **z**, **ch**, or **sh**, add **es**	
box	box**es**

3. For nouns that end with a consonant **y**, change the **y** to **i** and add **es**	
party	part**ies**

4. Learn and remember some irregular plurals	
child	children

Look at the ending of each **noun**. Make the **noun** plural and write it on the line.

1. computer _____

2. book _____

3. watch _____

4. goose _____

5. candy _____

6. boat _____

7. lily _____

8. fox _____

9. wish _____

10. sandwich _____

11. tree _____

12. box _____

13. ditch _____

14. quarry _____

15. table _____

16. swing _____

17. dish _____

18. freezer _____

19. inch _____

20. door _____

21. light _____

22. clubhouse _____

Pronouns are words that take the place of nouns.

<u>**Emily**</u> gave <u>**the books**</u> to <u>**Alex**</u>.

She gave **them** to **him**.

Subject Pronouns						
I	he	she	we	they	it	you

Read the sentences. Underline each **common noun** or **proper noun**.
Circle each **pronoun**.

1. The sunset was a shade of pinkish-orange. It was beautiful.

2. The sky was clear. It was blue.

3. The sailboats drifted on the water. They moved quickly.

4. Johnny wanted to go on the boat. Mom said it wasn't safe.

5. Johnny stayed at home. He played with his friend Billy.

6. Sam caught a fish. It was pretty big.

7. Sam struggled with the fish. Mom watched him.

8. Dad and Sam put the fish in a bucket. They brought it home.

9. The fish had a funny smell. It wasn't good.

10. Mom cooked the fish. Dad and Sam ate it.

Some **pronouns** take the place of nouns as the subject of the sentence.

       Lucy rode her bike to school.
       She rode her bike to school.

Write a **pronoun** that can take the place of the underlined noun.

1. _____ <u>Andrew</u> was supposed to wash the chalkboard.

2. _____ <u>Richard and I</u> are going to do it instead.

3. _____ <u>Jamie and Hannah</u> are in charge of cleaning the erasers.

4. _____ <u>The pencil sharpener</u> needed to be emptied.

5. _____ <u>Grace</u> emptied the trash.

6. _____ <u>Everyone in the class</u> pitched in to help.

7. _____ <u>Ted</u> took a message to the office.

8. _____ <u>Danny and Natalie</u> put books away in the library.

9. _____ <u>Our desks</u> were dirty, so we cleaned them.

10. _____ <u>The classroom</u> looked great when we were finished.

Name:_____ Date:_____

Some **pronouns** take the place of nouns that come after a verb.

The bus driver gave <u>the students</u> a treat
on the last day of school.
The bus driver gave **them** a treat
on the last day of school.

Object Pronouns

| me | you | him | her | it | us | them |

Write a **pronoun** that can take the place of the underlined noun.

1. _____ Janet called <u>Shelby</u> to invite her over to her house.

2. _____ The principal asked <u>Mrs. Jones</u> to bring her class first.

3. _____ Mrs. Cole spoke to <u>Brian</u> about using table manners.

4. _____ Leo shared <u>a birthday treat</u> with the whole class.

5. _____ My mom called <u>Billy and me</u> in for dinner.

6. _____ We got <u>the new CD</u> from the music store.

7. _____ We had fun playing <u>the computer game</u>.

8. _____ Grandma went to <u>the baseball game</u> with us.

9. _____ Lisa helped <u>her family</u> rearrange the furniture.

10. _____ Abby was crying because she hurt <u>her foot</u> on the sidewalk.

A **verb** in the present tense (or now) tells what a person or thing is doing.

Examples:
   For one person or thing, add **s** to the **verb**: The gorilla **pounds** on his chest.
   OR
   use **is** and add **ing** to the **verb**: The gorilla **is pounding** on his chest.

   For more than one, leave the **verb** as it is: The gorillas **pound** on their chests.
   OR
   use **are** and add **ing** to the **verb**: The gorillas **are pounding** on their chests.

Circle the **verbs** in each sentence.

1. The grizzly bear wanders into the cave.
2. We are watching the koala climb the tree.
3. The parrot journeys from one tree to another.
4. The zookeeper plays with the elephants.
5. The monkeys are acting silly today.
6. The seals glide through the water quickly.
7. The cheetah runs as fast as lightning.
8. We learned that the kangaroo uses its tail for balance.

 Challenge: Play *Verb Charades*! Write several action **verbs** on small cards. Put them in a pile face down or in a hat. Take turns picking cards and acting out the **verbs** without speaking. See who can guess the **verb** the quickest!

Write your own sentence using each **verb** below.

9. roar _____

   _____

10. sell _____

   _____

An action that was done in the past is often written as a **verb** that ends with the letters **ed**.

<u>Examples:</u> open**ed**, gallop**ed**, waddl**ed**, call**ed**, fasten**ed**, help**ed**

<u>Some Irregular Examples:</u> **went, had, left, flew, ran, ate, drove, fed, said, gave, knew**

Look at the underlined **verb** in each sentence. Rewrite each **verb** to show past tense.

1. Jackie <u>wish</u> that she had new crayons. _____

2. Harold <u>hope</u> to go to the concert last Saturday. _____

3. Juanita <u>want</u> to eat at the new restaurant, but it was not open yet. _____

4. Theresa <u>watch</u> her favorite show last night. _____

5. Tom <u>play</u> darts with me yesterday. _____

6. They <u>vacation</u> in Myrtle Beach five years ago. _____

7. Last week, I <u>crash</u> my bike into a tree. _____

An action that will happen in the future is often written as a **verb** with the word **will**.

<u>Examples:</u> He **will eat**.   She **will drink**.   They **will hop**.   It **will work**.

Write a complete sentence to answer the questions. Use the word **will** and an action **verb**.

8. What will you eat for dinner tomorrow?

_____

9. What will you do after dinner?

_____

10. What do you plan to do this summer?

_____

11. Which book do you plan to read next?

_____

12. What would you like to do this weekend?

_____

The **verb <u>to be</u>** joins the subject of the sentence with words that describe it. It tells what the subject is or what the condition of the subject is.

I **<u>am</u>** a girl.

I **<u>am</u>** happy.

Circle the *present tense* form of the **verb <u>to be</u>** in each sentence.

1. My cousin's birthday party is today.

2. He is nine years old.

3. I am nine years old, too.

4. My brother and I are excited.

5. His parties are usually a lot of fun.

Forms of the **verb <u>to be</u>**	
Present Tense	
I	am
he, she, it	is
you, we	are
Past Tense	
I, he, she, it	was
you, we	were

Write the correct *past tense* form of the **verb <u>to be</u>** to complete each sentence.

6. Miss Dawson _____ a teacher.

7. Arnold and Jack _____ on the same team last year.

8. The trip to the zoo _____ a great learning experience.

9. I _____ the youngest child in my family until my sister was born.

10. We _____ on our way out the door when the phone rang.

Name:_____   Date:_____

A word that helps the **main verb** tell what the subject is doing or did is called
a **helping verb**.

We **are learning** about animals.

helping verb   main verb

Examples:
has, have, had,
was, were,
am, are

Circle the **helping verbs** in each sentence.

1. We were told to research an animal.

2. Each student has selected an animal of interest.

3. I have learned about the tiger's eating habits and habitat.

4. Some students had researched the life cycle of their animal as well.

5. Some students had learned about how the animal defends itself.

Write a **helping verb** to complete each sentence.

6. Dad took us to the park before he _____ eaten his breakfast.

7. Jeff and I _____ been to the park before.

8. We _____ seen many interesting animals at the park.

9. I _____ going to ask Melanie to go next time.

10. We _____ hoping to go again next week.

Name:_____   Date:_____

Review: Nouns, Proper Nouns & Plural Nouns

Circle the **common nouns** and underline the **proper nouns** in each sentence.

1. My favorite months of the year are June and July.

2. Andrew and Alyssa stopped at the library after school.

3. Last Tuesday I helped my dad by cutting the grass and pulling weeds.

4. Her grandmother lives in New York City.

5. I saw the parade on North Creek Lane last Saturday.

Circle the **singular nouns** and underline the **plural nouns**.

6. Did you see the rabbits eating carrots in Mr. Farmer's garden?

7. Several deer ran across the trail as I was hiking in the park.

8. Have you seen my markers, pencils, and my sketch pad?

9. I'd rather have ten math problems than one story to write for an assignment.

10. The waves washed away our sandcastle and fort on the beach.

Rewrite each **singular noun** to make it plural.

11. ear _____   16. record _____

12. porcupine _____   17. eatery _____

13. carton _____   18. tax _____

14. daisy _____   19. fairy _____

15. pouch _____   20. pencil _____

Name:_____   Date:_____

Review: Pronouns

Circle the **pronouns** in each sentence.

1. We made pizza for dinner.

2. It tasted really good.

3. We added many ingredients to the pizza.

4. I wanted to put pepperoni on it.

5. Rick wanted to put extra cheese on it.

6. He also wanted sausage, but we didn't have any.

7. Dad said that he had a taste for mushrooms.

8. It was the best pizza I ever tasted.

9. Maybe we should open our own pizza shop.

10. It would probably be a lot of fun!

Write a **pronoun** that can take the place of the underlined nouns.

11. _____ <u>Rick and I</u> had fun making pizza.

12. _____ Dad helped us make <u>the pizza</u>.

13. _____ <u>Dad</u> had lots of fun, too.

14. _____ <u>My mom and sister</u> asked for a slice.

15. _____ <u>My sister</u> didn't like the mushrooms.

Name:_____ Date:_____

Review: Nouns & Verbs

Underline all the **nouns** and circle all the **verbs** in each sentence.

1. Our class took a field trip to the history museum yesterday morning.

2. We played word games and read our favorite books on the bus.

3. The group arrived at the impressive new building at 10:15.

4. The museum guides lead us around to each exhibit.

5. I enjoyed the field trip.

Challenge: Try this activity with a friend. Think of six people, machines, other animals, or objects and say a **verb** to describe what they do!

6. Amy and Andy Brown live in the house next to mine.

7. We pack picnic lunches and ride our bikes to the park.

8. After we eat lunch, the three of us look for interesting wild flowers.

9. Once we actually found the most incredible flowers growing under a fern.

10. Sometimes we hike for a while before we ride back home.

Write a **verb** to describe something each animal might do!

11. kangaroo _____   14. butterfly _____

12. cheetah _____   15. monkey _____

13. penguin _____   16. horse _____

Name:_____ Date:_____

Review: Nouns & Verbs

Read each sentence. Circle each **noun**. Draw a box around the **main verbs**. Underline each **helping verb**.

1. Yesterday, we were helping with yard work.

2. I was pulling weeds out of the flowerbeds.

3. Jackie and mom were planting flowers.

4. They had placed the dirt in the garden already.

5. The clouds grew dark, but it didn't rain.

6. We had fun helping each other!

7. The little girl was eating an enormous slice of pizza.

8. My grandma and I have baked delicious homemade brownies.

9. The sunset has made the evening quite romantic.

10. We have waited a long time for the movie to start!

STOP! TAKE A BREAK! You did a great job! Place your Book Mark here & RELAX!

Subjects and **verbs** must agree. If the **subject** is singular (just one), the **verb** has to be singular. If the **subject** is plural (more than one), the **verb** has to be plural.

Read the sentences. Circle the correct **verb** to finish each sentence.

1. My friend and I | **practice   practices** | for the soccer match.

2. Jilian | **know   knows** | where to find the best pizza!

3. The farmers | **ride rides** | huge tractors over the fields.

Tip:
Read the sentence out loud. If the verb sounds funny in the sentence, it's probably not the correct choice.

4. Those horses | **gallop   gallops** | on the muddy track.

5. A new family | **live   lives** | in that house on the corner.

6. We heard the scientists | **speak   speaks** | about the discovery.

7. Will that tiny ant really | **move   moves** | those crumbs?

8. Our teacher | **grade   grades** | our spelling tests right away.

9. I'd like to | **jump   jumps** | on the trampoline.

10. How did you | **learn   learns** | that poem so quickly?

11. She always | **bake   bakes** | muffins for breakfast.

12. Let's see if we can | **take   takes** | a walk later today.

Every sentence must have a **subject** and a **predicate**. The **subject** tells who or what is doing the action. The **predicate** tells what the subject does or is.

Tip:
Remember – Every sentence begins with a capital letter and ends with a period.

The dogs bark.
subject   predicate

Read each sentence. Draw one line under the **subject** and two lines under the **predicate**.

1. We organized a baseball game.

2. We played at the community park.

3. We won the game in an extra inning!

4. I thought the game would never be over.

5. Mom watched the game from the bleachers.

6. She cheered us on all afternoon!

7. The team had ice cream after the game.

8. I love ice cream as much as winning!

Every sentence has two main parts.

1. **Subject** or the **naming part** tells who or what a sentence is about.
2. **Predicate** or the **action part** tells what a subject is or does.

Lions roar.
subject   predicate

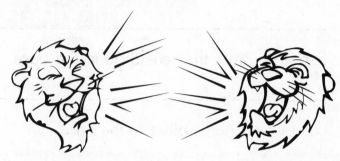

Read each sentence. Circle the **subject** and underline the **predicate**.

1.  Our class went on a field trip to the zoo.

2. We bought our tickets and went in through the front gate.

3. The teacher divided our class up into small groups.

4. I was in the group with my two best friends.

5. We went to see the koalas first.

6. Emma wanted to see the elephants next.

7. Our group stopped at a park bench to have a snack while we watched the giraffes.

8. Jeanie and Lily wanted to see the cheetahs.

9. Mrs. Johnson said it was time to meet our class back at the front entrance.

10. We learned a whole lot about the different animals we saw that day.

Name:_____   Date:_____

Rewrite each group of words to make it a complete sentence with a **subject** and a **predicate**.

1. went to the store to buy flowers

   Lena went to the store to buy flowers.

2. ben his mom if they could go to the store.

   _____

3. Lauren and her brother in the yard

   _____

4. is teaching her how to knit.

   _____

5. grandpa early to go fishing.

   _____

Write five complete sentences using the words in the box. Use each word or group of words once.

Gary and Michelle	Shelly and I	went to the library	took a boat to the island
Jonathan	We	played in the clubhouse	stood in line for an hour
The whole class		skated to my house	

6. _____

7. _____

8. _____

9. _____

10. _____

 Challenge: Find 5 newspaper headlines. If the headlines are not complete sentences, decide what is missing. Then, rewrite the headline to make it a complete sentence.

Write a **subject** from the list (or make up your own) to complete each sentence.

They	Martin
The principal	The aquarium
The truck	The Smiths
We	Alexis and Karen
Grandma and grandpa	Ashley
The pet shop	Jack and Alan

1. _____ walked home from school today.

2. _____ are on the same baseball team.

3. _____ earned an extra recess for excellent behavior.

4. _____ brought all the furniture to their new house.

5. _____ has practically every species of fish!

6. _____ played outside all day.

7. _____ built a new clubhouse in their backyard.

8. _____ ordered a new red car.

9. _____ thought they played their best game yet.

10. _____ watched a movie on Saturday afternoon.

Write a **predicate** from the list (or make up your own) to complete each sentence.

> went to the playground with her babysitter.
> broke when my brother threw it on the floor.
> planted a colorful bush in their garden.
> was having a huge sale.
> had fun at the parade.
> enjoyed the beautiful sunshine today.
> was playing my favorite song.
> is a healthy snack.
> was very relaxing.
> went to the pool for the day.

1. They _____

2. The toy _____

3. We _____

4. The radio _____

5. My family _____

6. Jessica _____

7. An apple _____

8. The vacation _____

9. The store _____

10. Their friends _____

Name:_____ Date:_____

Read each sentence. Circle the **subject** and underline the **predicate**.

1. Our family goes on a vacation every year.

2. The best vacation was when we went to Washington, D.C.

3. We saw so many historic sites.

4. My favorite part was the tour of the White House.

Write a **subject** to complete each sentence.

5. _____ went to the library.

6. _____ and I ride bicycles together.

7. _____ was late getting to work yesterday.

8. _____ sells three flavors of ice cream.

Write a **predicate** to complete each sentence.

9. The man _____.

10. Jerry and Jason _____.

11. Natalie _____.

12. The boat _____.

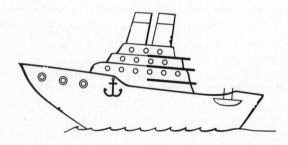

Tip:
A **predicate**
should have an **action
verb** or a
***to be* verb** in it
(i.e. is, am, are,
was, were).

Review: Editing Sentences

Rewrite each group of words to make a complete and correct sentence with a **subject** and **predicate**.

1. the playground went to I

   _____

2. My aunt at the clothing store works

   _____

3. monkey on the swing Do you see the

   _____

4. movie Lynn and I on Saturday saw a

   _____

5. two big dogs next live door

   _____

6. My favorite checkers game is

   _____

7. driving a red bird saw my father while to work

   _____

8. got wet socks my

   _____

9. We decided to baseball play

   _____

10. home for a snack I came

   _____

Name:_____   Date:_____

Review: Editing Sentences

Rewrite the sentences with the correct punctuation, spelling, and grammar.

1. her new haircut is much shoreter?

   _____

2. I is so happy that it is mine birfday

   _____

3. It is n't time two go too the store yet

   _____

4. please hang up your clothes jacket and umbrella and put yer toy's away.

   _____

5. Ware were you yester day!

   _____

6. They bawght a new car that'is red, green and wite

   _____

7. When mom get hoMe i need to ask her a qestion?

   _____

8. how long did it take he to makes that cake?

   _____

9. This game was confusing because it does'nt has directions.

   _____

10. do you's need anything from there store?

   _____

Name:_____ Date:_____

Review: Editing Sentences

Rewrite the sentence or sentences with the correct punctuation, spelling, and grammar.

1. I like too play baseball in the bulldogs team?

   _____

2. I goed to the feeld but th game, were cancelled, because of rane

   _____

3. john be sad becausehe want to try out her new baseball glove.

   _____

4. When we leaved the field, Dad asked do we wanted to stop four icecream?

   _____

5. we got's to order a sundaes or a cones.

   _____

6. I ordering a duble scoop of chalkate and Dad ordering vanilla!

   _____

7. We eight at a picnic table that, was, reelly. Long,

   _____

8. It's was time to go so wee thanked dad!

   _____

9. On the way home, we talked about we talked about basket ball, and, baseball

   _____

STOP! **TAKE A BREAK!** You did a great job! **Place your Book Mark here & RELAX!**

Name:_____   Date:_____

Make a list of five things that make you feel happy.

1. _____

2. _____

3. _____

4. _____

5. _____

Choose one of the things from your list and write a few sentences about it on the lines below. Be sure to explain why it makes you feel happy and give as many details as you can!

_____

_____

_____

_____

_____

_____

_____

_____

_____

_____

_____

_____

_____

Writing notes, journals, and lists

Name:_____   Date:_____

Write a letter to a friend using the prompts below.

Date _____

Dear _____,

     Did you ever wonder what you would do if you had a million dollars? Here's what

I would do. First, _____.

_____

_____

_____.

Then, _____

_____

_____.

Finally, _____

_____

_____.

_____. Please write back soon

and tell me what you would do! _____

_____

_____.

Sincerely,

_____

Read the story and respond to the questions on the next page.

Sugar and Spice

Once a week, Michelle and Ryan stopped by the pet shop on their way home from school. They stopped for two reasons—Sugar and Spice. Sugar and Spice were two kittens that shared a cage. They played so nicely together. Michelle and Ryan both had been begging their parents for a kitten. Since they are neighbors, they thought it would be perfect if Michelle got Sugar and Ryan got Spice.

Things got busy at school and home, so Michelle and Ryan didn't have time to stop by the pet shop. How they missed seeing Sugar and Spice! A few weeks later, Michelle and her mom passed by the pet shop. To Michelle's surprise, she didn't see Spice in the front window. She only saw Sugar. A terrible thought crossed her mind. Maybe someone bought Spice and the two best friends would never be together again. She went home practically in tears, but her mom assured her everything would be okay.

That weekend was Ryan's birthday party. Michelle was really looking forward to going because Ryan's parties were always fun. At the party they played games, sang, and ate cake and ice cream. Then came the best part—the presents! Ryan got lots of neat toys, including a few that Michelle was planning to put on her own birthday list. Just when Ryan thought he was done opening all the presents, his dad brought out a small box with holes in it and a bow on top. Ryan carefully opened the box and found Spice inside!

Ryan had mixed feelings. He was excited to have a new kitten, but he was also sad that Spice was not with his best friend Sugar anymore. Ryan's parents sensed his sad feeling and motioned for Michelle's mom. She stepped forward with a small box with holes in it and a bow on top. The box looked just like the one that Ryan got. Michelle's mom asked Michelle if she wanted an early birthday present. But before Michelle could answer, Ryan had the box open and Sugar was peeking out! Sugar and Spice immediately started playing together and Ryan looked at Michelle and said, "This is the best birthday ever!"

Name:_____   Date:_____

Think about the story *Sugar and Spice* from the previous page. Write your personal responses to the questions below. Use complete sentences.

1. Do you think Sugar and Spice will continue to be best friends? Why or why not?

_____

_____

2. What was your favorite part in the story? Describe it.

_____

_____

3. Explain how you think they felt when they saw Sugar and Spice together again.

_____

_____

4. Describe how you think Ryan's feelings changed after Michelle opened her early birthday present.

_____

_____

5. Who do you think is happier, Ryan and Michelle or Sugar and Spice? Why?

_____

_____

6. How would you feel if you received a gift like Sugar or Spice?

_____

_____

7. If you could get a special pet of your own, what kind of animal would you like and why?

_____

_____

Think about an exciting time that you shared with a family member, such as going camping with Grandpa, going to a concert with Mom, or visiting an amusement park with your cousin. Write your special moment on the line.

My exciting moment is:

_____

Write some details about your exciting moment in the box.

Tip:
Try to create pictures in your mind of what you saw, smelled, touched, heard, tasted, or how you felt. Then, use words to help recreate that for the reader!

Write a paragraph (or several sentences) about your exciting moment using the supporting details that you wrote in the box.

_____

_____

_____

_____

_____

_____

_____

_____

_____

Name:_____ Date:_____

Review: Writing

Write a **noun, verb,** or **compound word** on each blank space to create your own story! Look below each line so you know what kind of word to write. Then, read your story.

Last Halloween, I decided to dress up as a _____.
                                                          noun

My best friend, _____, dressed as a _____.
                  proper noun/name   noun

The evening was cold and dark. We _____ and
                                              verb

_____ down the street until we came to the _____ on
    verb   noun

the corner. The _____ was piled high around the front door and no lights
                 plural noun

were on. Suddenly, we heard a sound coming from the _____.
                                                      compound word

We almost _____ right on the spot!
             verb

Luckily, my friend had a flashlight! We aimed it at the _____
                                                        compound word

and _____ when we realized it was only a
              verb

_____. I couldn't believe it! We were so relieved that we _____.
    noun   verb

Once we had our fill of _____, we _____ back
                          noun   verb

home. Our treat bags were loaded with _____. I can hardly
                                        plural noun

wait for Halloween next year!

Name:_____   Date:_____

Review: Writing

Think about your favorite animal and what might happen if that animal lived with you. Write a short story about this silly idea.

Title: _____

Beginning: _____

_____

Tip: Capitalize the first letters in your title. Be sure to use complete sentences in your story!

_____

_____

_____

Middle: _____

_____

_____

_____

_____

End: _____

_____

_____

_____

_____

STOP! **TAKE A BREAK!** **You did a great job!** Place your Book Mark here & RELAX!

Answer Key

Please take time to review the work your child or student has completed. Remember to praise both success and effort. If your child makes a mistake, let him or her know that mistakes are a part of learning. Explain why the incorrect response was not the best choice. Then, encourage your child to think it through and select a better choice.

page 3

page 4
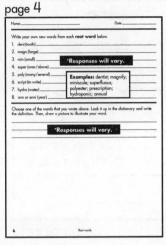

page 5

page 6

page 7
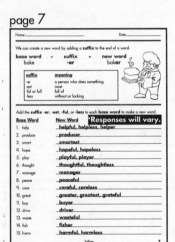

page 8
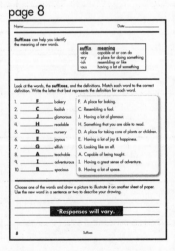

page 9
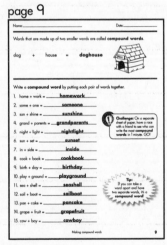

page 10
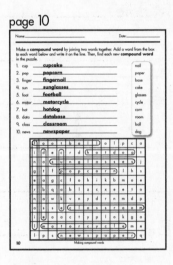

page 11
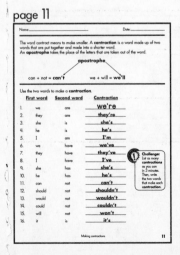

page 12
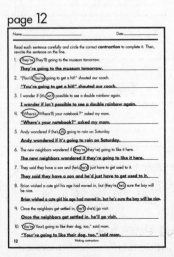

page 13
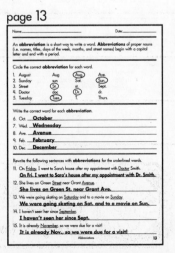

page 14

page 15

Review: Compound Words, Contractions & Abbreviations

Circle all the **compound words**, underline the **abbreviations**, and draw a box around the **contractions** in the paragraphs below.

Noises in the Night

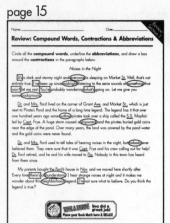

Review: Compound Words, Contractions & Abbreviations   15

---

page 16

Use a **comma** to separate words in a **series** of three or more things.

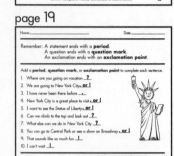

I packed my **shirt, pants, and socks.**

Remember to place a **comma** after each word in a series, including the word that is just before "and" or "or."

Read each sentence. Add **commas** where they belong.

1. We went to the beach and took our sunscreen, towels, shovels, and pails.
2. My mom bought strawberries, peaches, and watermelon for a healthy snack.
3. We played volleyball, tossed the Frisbee, and built a sand castle.
4. The days were fun, exciting, and tiring!
5. When it was time to go, we shook the sand out of our towels, blankets, and clothes.
6. On the first day of school, I brought my school supplies, book bag, and lunch box.
7. We talked about our activities, our daily schedule, and what we would learn this year.
8. Our teacher told us to read, study math facts, and share our thoughts about the first day with our family.
9. I can't wait to learn about multiplication, division, and fractions!
10. I think school is going to be challenging, exciting, and fun.

Write a sentence about three or more of your favorite foods and snacks. Don't forget the commas!

"Responses will vary.

Examples: My favorite snacks are popcorn, peanut butter and chocolate ice cream, and potato chips.

16   Using commas in a series

---

page 17

Use a **comma** between the name of a city and state, and between the day and year.

I live in **Columbus, Ohio.**
We moved here on **July 28, 2001.**

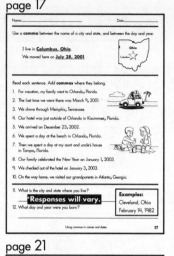

Read each sentence. Add **commas** where they belong.

1. For vacation, my family went to Orlando, Florida.
2. The last time we were there was March 9, 2001.
3. We drove through Memphis, Tennessee.
4. Our hotel was just outside of Orlando in Kissimmee, Florida.
5. We arrived on December 23, 2002.
6. We spent a day at the beach in Orlando, Florida.
7. Then we spent a day at my aunt and uncle's house in Tampa, Florida.
8. Our family celebrated the New Year on January 1, 2003.
9. We checked out of the hotel on January 3, 2003.
10. On the way home, we visited our grandparents in Atlanta, Georgia.

11. What is the city and state where you live?
"Responses will vary.
12. What day and year were you born?

Examples: Cleveland, Ohio February 14, 1982

Using commas in names and dates   17

---

page 18

Every sentence begins with a **capital letter** and ends with a **punctuation mark**.

The party starts at 6:30. — A **statement** tells something and ends with a period.

What time is it? — A **question** asks something and ends with a question mark.

Let's go! — An **exclamation** shows strong feeling and ends with an exclamation point.

Circle the number before the sentences that are not written correctly. Rewrite the sentences that are not written correctly.

1. my sister and I went to Lauren's party.
My sister and I went to Lauren's party.
2. Then Lauren opened her presents
Then Lauren opened her presents.
3. can you guess what she got
Can you guess what she got?
4. Lauren's mom gave her a dress.
Lauren's mom gave her a dress.
5. After the gifts were opened, we had cake.
6. the cake was chocolate – my favorite!
The cake was chocolate – my favorite!
7. When we finished our cake, do you know what we played
When we finished our cake, do you know what we played?
8. i won a prize for the ring toss game.
I won a prize for the ring toss game.
9. It was a great party
It was a great party!

18   Using periods, question marks, exclamation marks, and apostrophes

---

page 19

Remember: A statement ends with a **period.**
A question ends with a **question mark.**
An exclamation ends with an **exclamation point.**

Add a **period, question mark, or exclamation point** to complete each sentence.

1. Where are you going on vacation?
2. We are going to New York City, or!
3. I have never been there before.
4. New York City is a great place to visit, or!
5. I want to see the Statue of Liberty, or!
6. Can we climb to the top and look out?
7. What else can we do in New York City?
8. You can go to Central Park or see a show on Broadway, or!
9. That sounds like so much fun!
10. I can't wait.

11. Write a **statement.**
"Responses will vary.
12. Write a **question.**

Examples: **statement:** Hippos are big. **question:** What is your favorite animal?
13. Write an **exclamation.** **exclamation:** I can't get my new pet!

Using periods, question marks, exclamation marks, and apostrophes   19

---

page 20

Cross out each mistake you see in the sentences below. Rewrite each sentence with correct capitalization and punctuation.

1. i cant wait to go to the basketball game tonight?
I can't wait to go to the basketball game tonight!
2. I am excited to be able to go to the championship game.
I am excited to be able to go to the championship game.
3. its girls' night, so I will be going with molly Megan and margaret
It's girls' night, so I will be going with Molly, Megan, and Margaret.
4. Do you think I should wear my red blue and gold jersey or my white t-shirt
Do you think I should wear my red, blue, and gold jersey or my white t-shirt?
5. our seats are up really high, but the view is very good!
Our seats are up really high, but the view is very good! (or !)
6. My favorite player really knows how to slam dunk
My favorite player really knows how to slam dunk. (or !)
7. I usually get a snack at the game like peanuts popcorn or a hotdog
I usually get a snack at the game like peanuts, popcorn, or a hotdog.
8. When I get a large drink I get to keep the souvenir cup
When I get a large drink I get to keep the souvenir cup.
9. Do you know how many fans can fit in the arena
Do you know how many fans can fit in the arena?
10. who is your favorite player.
Who is your favorite player?
11. Last time we went to the game I got a banner a rally towel and a t-shirt
Last time we went to the game I got a banner, a rally towel, and a t-shirt (or)
12. do you think our team will score more than 100 points
Do you think our team will score more than 100 points?

20   Using punctuation correctly

---

page 21

Rewrite each **singular noun** below so that it is a **plural noun**, or meaning more than one. Then, draw a picture to show one of the plural nouns.

1. computer — **computers**
2. cell phone — **cell phones**
3. party — **parties**
4. radio — **radios**
5. goat — **goats**
6. guinea pig — **guinea pigs**
7. fry — **fries**
8. pie — **pies**
9. candy — **candies**
10. daisy — **daisies**
11. dish — **dishes**
12. fox — **foxes**
13. sock — **socks**
14. kiss — **kisses**
15. kitty — **kitties**
16. city — **cities**
17. page — **pages**
18. pastry — **pastries**
19. radish — **radishes**
20. tax — **taxes**

Tip: Remember — if a word ends in the letter y, the plural **noun** will end in ies.

Challenge: Try these plural word riddles:
1. What has 4 wheels and flies?
2. What did the frog order at the fast food restaurant?

Riddle Answers:
A garbage truck!
A burger and flies!

"Responses will vary. Drawing must show more than 1 object.

Spelling singular and plural nouns   21

---

page 22

Circle each word that is spelled incorrectly. Rewrite the words correctly on the lines below each sentence.

1. Brenda felt like an ugly duckling because she had a pimple on her nose.
ugly   because
2. It was a beautiful day for flying kites.
beautiful   flying
3. How neatly can you write your name backwards without looking?
neatly   looking
4. When we entered the restaurant, the waitress was not that friendly.
entered   friendly
5. We wanted to order some soft drinks, but the waitress was not being helpful.
wanted   helpful
6. Sarah was hoping to see the game live, but she was grateful that it was on TV.
hoping   grateful
7. Basketball players are talented and very powerful.
talented   powerful
8. Because of the construction, traffic was moving very slowly.
moving   slowly
9. I had trouble hearing my friend's message because she was rambling too quickly.
hearing   quickly
10. I climbed the hill without much difficulty.
climbed   difficulty
11. Patrick joined the soccer team late, but he is still playing a lot.
joined   playing
12. She is certainly welcome to come with you, if she will speak quietly.
certainly   quietly
13. We wanted it to be a surprise, but he was watching when we came in the cake.
wanted   watching

22   Spelling words with common suffixes and endings

---

page 23

Circle the word in each word pair that is spelled correctly.

1. abowt / **about**   beter / **better**   brieng / **bring**   carn / **carie**
2. **cleen** / cleen   cut / **cut**   dun / **dun**   **draw** / drow
3. **drink** / dreenk   **eight** / aight   fawl / **fall**   **far** / farr
4. fuvl / **full**   **got** / gowt   growd / **growed**   **hold** / holled
5. **hot** / hawt   **hurt** / hert   iff / **if**   **keep** / keep
6. **kind** / kined   **laff** / laugh   liegt / **light**   **long** / long
7. **much** / mooch   **myself** / miself   **never** / nevr   **only** / onlee
8. **owne** / own   **pick** / pik   **seven** / sehvin   **small** / smoll
9. **show** / shaow   **six** / sicks   **small** / smoll   **start** / stahrt
10. tenn / **ten**   **today** / todae   togethr / **together**   trie / **try**

Choose 3 correctly spelled words from above and use them in a sentence. Draw a picture to go with your sentence.

11.
12.
13.

"Responses will vary.

Spelling common words correctly   23

---

page 24

Read each sentence. Add **commas, periods, question marks,** or **exclamation marks** where they belong.

1. For my birthday I am having a party with my family, friends, and neighbors.
2. I invited Ian, Adam, and Eric.
3. Are Robbie, Joseph, and Noah coming, too?
4. What are we having for lunch?
5. Yeah, I love ice cream!
6. What is your favorite kind of ice cream?
7. Parties are great!
8. Is this present from Mom, Dad, and Bobby?
9. We are having hamburgers, cheeseburgers, and hotdogs.
10. I love cheeseburgers with ketchup, mustard, and pickles! or.
11. Dad likes his with lettuce, onions, and tomatoes, too.
12. We are also having potato salad, baked beans, and pasta salad.
13. Dessert will be strawberry, chocolate, and vanilla ice cream.
14. We are going to play volleyball, have a water balloon toss, and go swimming.
15. You need to take your time, throw carefully, and concentrate on the balloon toss.
16. I am looking forward to opening my gifts, eating, and playing with my friends.
17. Aunt Betty, Aunt Rose, and Uncle Len each brought a present for me.
18. I am really hoping to get a new bike, a helmet, and a raft for the pool.
19. Family, friends, and neighbors can have a lot of fun together.

Using punctuation correctly   24

---

page 25

Rewrite each sentence using capital letters and the correct **punctuation.**

1. guess what   yesterday we went to the swimming pool
Guess what?   Yesterday, we went to the swimming pool.
2. jeff ashley and i got really tired from swimming a lot
Jeff, Ashley, and I got really tired from swimming a lot.
3. I swam so much I took a nap when we got home
I swam so much I took a nap when we got home.
4. What was the best part   the best part was the water slide
What was the best part?   The best part was the water slide.
5. the line for the twirly twister was long   that's my favorite ride
The line for the Twirly Tister was long.   That's my favorite ride!
6. the diving board was exciting, too   it's so high up
The diving board was exciting, too!   It's so high up!
7. can ashley dive from the high board   absolutely she is a great diver
Can Ashley dive from the high board?   Absolutely, she is a great diver!
8. mom brought healthy snacks for us to eat
Mom brought healthy snacks for us to eat.
9. the snacks helped give us energy so we could ride the super slide
The snacks helped give us energy so we could ride the Super Slide.
10. i liked the granola bars pretzels and carrot sticks
I liked the granola bars, pretzels, and carrot sticks.

Using punctuation correctly   25

---

page 26

Review: Punctuation & Spelling

Read each paragraph below. Cross out all **capitalizing** mistakes, **misspelled** words, or incorrect **punctuation.** Above each mistake, write the correct letter, word, or punctuation.

Corrected paragraphs:

The giant panda is a fascinating animal. It lives, eats and plays in China in the mountains and it uses its special paws to eat bamboo. The giant panda population is getting smaller because the panda has been hunted for fur and accidentally killed in traps set for other animals. The people of China have set up areas for pandas to live in safely. Also, it is against the law to hunt the giant panda.

Pizza is my favorite dinner. It is a healthy food! One reason is because it has vegetables on it. It usually has crust, spices, tomato sauce, and cheese. It can also have meat and vegetables like pepperoni, sausage, and mushrooms. What kind of pizza do you like?

26   **Review: Punctuation & Spelling**

---

page 27

Review: Punctuation & Spelling

Cross out any **misspelled** words, letters that should be **capitalized,** or **punctuation** that is incorrect. Above each mistake, write in the correct word, capital letter, or **punctuation.**   **Corrected sentences:**

1. Making Martha's Super Chocolate Chip Cookies can be a lot of fun!
2. First, preheat the oven to 350 degrees, grease the cookie sheets, and get out the ingredients.
3. Mix butter-flavored shortening, brown sugar, and white sugar in a bowl until light and fluffy.
4. Then, add the eggs one at a time and beat them well while stirring in vanilla.
5. Mix in the flour, baking soda, and salt slowly stir until creamy.
6. Finally, fold in the chocolate chips.
7. Now you are ready to drop the cookie dough onto the cookie sheets.
8. Bake the cookies for 8 to 10 minutes, or until light brown.
9. When they are done baking, allow the cookies to cool on the baking sheet for 5 minutes.
10. Then, move them to a wire rack to cool completely.
11. Enjoy your homemade treats!
12. Write two or three correct sentences about your favorite cookies!

"Responses will vary.

Review: Punctuation & Spelling   27

---

page 28

Review: Punctuation & Spelling

Cross out any **misspelled** words or incorrect **punctuation.** Above the mistakes, write in the correctly **spelled** words and the correct **punctuation.**   **Corrected sentences:**

1. Reading is important for many reasons.
2. It helps you to learn new things.
3. Reading is fun! (or)
4. Nathan likes to read mysteries, fiction, and action adventures.
5. You can pick up a book and take an adventure, go on a journey, or meet new friends.
6. You can read books like John's Summer Day, Michelle's Sneezing Problem, and Sheri's Big Win.
7. Recycling helps make our world a healthier and safer place.
8. Paul recycles plastic, aluminum, and paper.
9. You can reuse items to make crafts, games, or toys.
10. We have a limited amount of space on Earth. It helps to recycle.
11. So we should recycle as much as we can! (or)

28   Review: Punctuation & Spelling

---

page 29

Review: Punctuation & Spelling

Read each paragraph. Cross out all the mistakes you see on each line. Above the mistakes, write in the correctly **spelled** words, **capital letters,** or **punctuation.**   **Corrected paragraphs:**

Have you ever wondered about flying insects, butterflies, and moths? Did you know that there are many differences between butterflies and moths? First, butterflies are usually brightly colored with yellow, orange, red, and blue. Moths are usually dull in color. Second, butterflies are active during the day and moths are active at night. Third, butterflies form a chrysalis and moths form a cocoon.

Do you want to learn how to be a great cook? For an appetizer, you can make stuffed mushrooms, cheese and crackers, or onion rings. If you like chicken, you may want to make chicken soup, chicken dumplings, or chicken parmesan. If you prefer vegetarian dishes, you can learn how to make stir-fry with snow peas, carrots, and cabbage. For dessert, you might try chocolate pudding, fresh bread with jelly, or fruit salad. Enjoy your yummy treats!

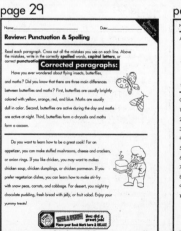

Review: Punctuation & Spelling   29

---

page 30

A **common noun** names a non-specific person, place, or thing.

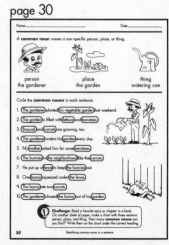

person — the gardener   place — the garden   thing — watering can

Circle the **common nouns** in each sentence.

1. The gardener planted his vegetable garden last weekend.
2. The garden is filled with lettuce and tomatoes.
3. Broccoli and carrots are growing, too.
4. The gardener waters his garden every day.
5. My mother asked him for some tomatoes.
6. The bunnies in the neighborhood like the carrots.
7. He put up a fence to keep the bunnies out.
8. One bunny squeezed under the fence.
9. The bunny ate two carrots.
10. The gardener chased the bunny out of his garden.

Challenge: Read a favorite story or chapter in a book. On another sheet of paper, make a chart with three sections: person, place, and thing. How many **common nouns** can you find? Write them on the chart under the correct heading.

30   Identifying common nouns in a sentence

Answers

page 31

Name: Date:

A **proper noun** names a specific person, place, or thing. **Proper nouns** always begin with a capital letter.

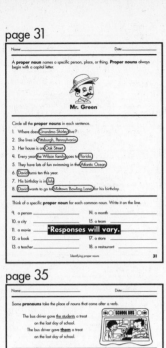

Mr. Green

Circle all the **proper nouns** in each sentence.

1. Where does Grandma Shirley live?
2. She lives in Pittsburgh, Pennsylvania.
3. Her house is on Oak Street.
4. Every year the Wilson family goes to Florida.
5. They have lots of fun swimming in the Atlantic Ocean.
6. David turns ten this year.
7. His birthday is in July.
8. David wants to go to Midtown Bowling Lanes for his birthday.

Think of a specific **proper noun** for each common noun. Write it on the line.

9. a person 14. a month
10. a city 15. a team
11. a movie 16. a toy
12. a book 17. a store
13. a teacher 18. a restaurant

*Responses will vary.

Identifying proper nouns 31

page 32

Name: Date:

A noun that names more than one person, place, or thing is called a **plural noun**.

There are four different ways to make a **plural noun**.

1. For most nouns, add **s**		2. For nouns that end in **x, z, ch,** or **sh**, add **es**	
hat	hats	box	boxes
3. For nouns that end with a consonant **y**, change the **y** to **i** and add **es**		4. Learn and remember some irregular plurals	
party	parties	child	children

Look at the ending of each **noun**. Make the **noun** plural and write it on the line.

1. computer **computers** 12. box **boxes**
2. book **books** 13. ditch **ditches**
3. watch **watches** 14. quarry **quarries**
4. goose **geese** 15. table **tables**
5. candy **candies** 16. swing **swings**
6. boat **boats** 17. dish **dishes**
7. lily **lilies** 18. freezer **freezers**
8. fox **foxes** 19. inch **inches**
9. wish **wishes** 20. door **doors**
10. sandwich **sandwiches** 21. light **lights**
11. tree **trees** 22. clubhouse **clubhouses**

32 Making nouns plural

page 33

Name: Date:

Pronouns are words that take the place of nouns.

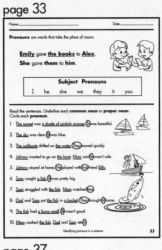

Emily gave **the books** to **Alex**.
She gave **them** to **him**.

Subject Pronouns					
I	he	she	we	they	it	you

Read the sentences. Underline each **common noun** or **proper noun**. Circle each **pronoun**.

1. The sunset was a shade of pinkish orange. It was beautiful.
2. The sky was clear. It was blue.
3. The sailboats drifted on the water. They moved quickly.
4. Johnny wanted to go on the boat. Mom said it wasn't safe.
5. Johnny stayed at home. He played with his friend Billy.
6. Sam caught a fish. It was pretty big.
7. Sam struggled with the fish. Mom watched him.
8. Dad and Sam put the fish in a bucket. They brought it home.
9. The fish had a funny smell. It wasn't good.
10. Mom cooked the fish. Dad and Sam ate it.

Identifying pronouns in a sentence 33

page 34

Name: Date:

Some **pronouns** take the place of nouns as the subject of the sentence.

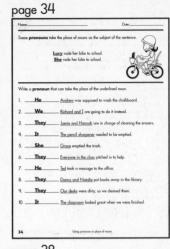

Lucy rode her bike to school.
She rode her bike to school.

Write a **pronoun** that can take the place of the underlined noun.

1. **He** Andrew was supposed to wash the chalkboard.
2. **We** Richard and I are going to do it instead.
3. **They** Jamie and Hannah are in charge of cleaning the erasers.
4. **It** The pencil sharpener needed to be emptied.
5. **She** Grace emptied the trash.
6. **They** Everyone in the class pitched in to help.
7. **He** Ted took a message to the office.
8. **They** Danny and Natalie put books away in the library.
9. **They** Our desks were dirty, so we cleaned them.
10. **It** The classroom looked great when we were finished.

34 Using pronouns in place of nouns

page 35

Name: Date:

Some **pronouns** take the place of nouns that come after a verb.

The bus driver gave the students a treat on the last day of school.
The bus driver gave them a treat on the last day of school.

SCHOOL BUS

Object Pronouns						
me	you	him	her	it	us	them

Write a **pronoun** that can take the place of the underlined noun.

1. **her** Janet called Shelby to invite her over to her house.
2. **her** The principal asked Mrs. Jones to bring her class first.
3. **him** Mrs. Cole spoke to Brian about using table manners.
4. **it** Leo shared a birthday treat with the whole class.
5. **us** My mom called Billy and me in for dinner.
6. **it** We got the new CD from the music store.
7. **it** We had fun playing the computer game.
8. **it** Grandma went to the baseball game with us.
9. **them** Lisa helped her family rearrange the furniture.
10. **it** Abby was crying because she hurt her foot on the sidewalk.

Using pronouns in place of nouns 35

page 36

Name: Date:

A **verb** in the present tense (or now) tells what a person or thing is doing.

Examples:
For one person or thing, add **s** to the **verb**: The gorilla **pounds** on his chest.
OR
use **is** and add **ing** to the **verb**: The gorilla **is pounding** on his chest.

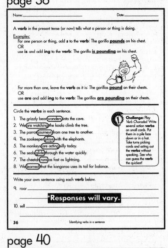

For more than one, leave the **verb** as it is: The gorillas **pound** on their chests.
OR
use **are** and add **ing** to the **verb**: The gorillas **are pounding** on their chests.

Circle the **verbs** in each sentence.

1. The grizzly bear wanders into the cave.
2. We are watching the koala climb the tree.
3. The parrot journeys from one tree to another.
4. The zookeeper plays with the elephants.
5. The monkeys are acting silly today.
6. The seals glide through the water quickly.
7. The cheetah runs as fast as lightning.
8. We learned that the kangaroo uses its tail for balance.

Challenge: Play *Verb Charades!* Write several action **verbs** on small cards. Put them in a pile face down or in a hat. Take turns picking cards and acting out the **verbs** without speaking. See who can guess the **verb** the quickest!

Write your own sentence using each **verb** below.

9. roar
10. sell

*Responses will vary.

36 Identifying verbs in a sentence

page 37

Name: Date:

An action that was done in the past is often written as a **verb** that ends with the letters **ed**.
Examples: opened, galloped, waddled, called, fastened, helped
Some Irregular Examples: **went, had, left, flew, ran, ate, drove, fed, said, gave, knew**

Look at the underlined **verb** in each sentence. Rewrite each **verb** to show past tense.

1. Jackie wish that she had new crayons. **wished**
2. Harold hope to go to the concert last Saturday. **hoped**
3. Juanita want to eat at the new restaurant, but it was not open yet. **wanted**
4. Theresa watch her favorite show last night. **watched**
5. Tom play darts with me yesterday. **played**
6. They vacation in Myrtle Beach five years ago. **vacationed**
7. Last week, I crash my bike into a tree. **crashed**

An action that will happen in the future is often written as a **verb** with the word **will**.
Examples: He **will eat**. She **will drink**. They **will hop**. It **will work**.

Write a complete sentence to answer the questions. Use the word **will** and an action **verb**.

8. What will you eat for dinner tomorrow?
I will eat macaroni and cheese.
9. What will you do after dinner?
I will watch my favorite movie.
10. What do you plan to do this summer? *Responses will vary.
I will visit my sister in Seattle.
11. Which book do you plan to read next?
I will read Madilyn's New Blanket.
12. What would you like to do this weekend?
I will ride a roller coaster at the fair this weekend.

Past and future tense of verbs 37

page 38

Name: Date:

The **verb to be** joins the subject of the sentence with words that describe it. It tells what the subject is or what the condition of the subject is.

I **am** a girl.
I **am** happy.

Circle the *present tense* form of the **verb to be** in each sentence.

1. My cousin's birthday party is today.
2. He is nine years old.
3. I am nine years old, too.
4. My brother and I are excited.
5. His parties are usually a lot of fun.

Forms of the **verb to be**	
Present Tense	
I	am
he, she, it	is
you, we	are
Past Tense	
I, he, she, it	was
you, we	were

Write the correct *past tense* form of the **verb to be** to complete each sentence.

6. Miss Dawson **was** a teacher.
7. Arnold and Jack **were** on the same team last year.
8. The trip to the zoo **was** a great learning experience.
9. I **was** the youngest child in my family until my sister was born.
10. We **were** on our way out the door when the phone rang.

38 Using the present and past tense form of the verb to be

page 39

Name: Date:

A word that helps the **main verb** tell what the subject is doing or did is called a **helping verb**.

We **are learning** about animals.
helping verb main verb

Examples:
has, have, had, was, were, am, are

Circle the **helping verbs** in each sentence.

1. We were told to research an animal.
2. Each student has selected an animal of interest.
3. So, I have learned about the tiger's eating habits and habitat.
4. Some students had researched the life cycle of their animal as well.
5. Some students had learned about how the animal defends itself.

Write a **helping verb** to complete each sentence.

6. Dad took us to the park before he **had** eaten his breakfast.
7. Jeff and I **had** been to the park before.
8. We **had** seen many interesting animals at the park.
9. I **am** going to ask Melanie to go next time.
10. We **are** hoping to go again next week.

Using helping verbs 39

page 40

Review Section 3

Name: Date:

Review: Nouns, Proper Nouns & Plural Nouns

Circle the **common nouns** and underline the **proper nouns** in each sentence.

1. My favorite months of the year are June and July.
2. Andrew and Alyssa stopped at the library after school.
3. Last Tuesday I helped my dad by cutting the grass and pulling weeds.
4. Her grandmother lives in New York City.
5. I saw the parade on North Creek Lane last Saturday.

Circle the **singular nouns** and underline the **plural nouns**.

6. Did you see the rabbits eating carrots in Mr. Farmer's garden?
7. Several deer ran across the trail as I was hiking in the park.
8. Have you seen my markers, pencils, and my sketch pad?
9. I'd rather have ten math problems than one story to write for an assignment.
10. The waves washed away our sandcastle and fort on the beach.

Rewrite each **singular noun** to make it plural.

11. ear **ears** 16. record **records**
12. porcupine **porcupines** 17. eatery **eateries**
13. carton **cartons** 18. tax **taxes**
14. daisy **daisies** 19. fairy **fairies**
15. pouch **pouches** 20. pencil **pencils**

40 Review: Nouns, Proper Nouns & Plural Nouns

page 41

Review Section 3

Name: Date:

Review: Pronouns

Circle the **pronouns** in each sentence.

1. We made pizza for dinner.
2. It tasted really good.
3. We added many ingredients to the pizza.
4. I wanted to put pepperoni on it.
5. Rick wanted to put extra cheese on it.
6. He also wanted sausage, but we didn't have any.
7. Dad said that he had a taste for mushrooms.
8. It was the best pizza I ever tasted.
9. Maybe we should open our own pizza shop.
10. It would probably be a lot of fun!

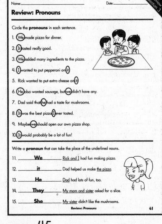

Write a **pronoun** that can take the place of the underlined nouns.

11. **We** Rick and I had fun making pizza.
12. **it** Dad helped us make the pizza.
13. **He** Dad had lots of fun, too.
14. **They** My mom and sister asked for a slice.
15. **She** My sister didn't like the mushrooms.

Review: Pronouns 41

page 42

Review Section 3

Name: Date:

Review: Nouns & Verbs

Underline all the **nouns** and circle all the **verbs** in each sentence.

1. Our class took a field trip to the history museum yesterday morning.
2. We played word games and read our favorite books on the bus.
3. The group arrived at the impressive new building at 10:15.
4. The museum guides lead us around to each exhibit.
5. I enjoyed the field trip.
6. Amy and Andy Brown live in the house next to mine.
7. We pack picnic lunches and ride our bikes to the park.
8. After we eat lunch, the three of us look for interesting wild flowers.
9. Once we actually found the most incredible flowers growing under a fern.
10. Sometimes we hike for a while before we ride back home.

Challenge: Try this activity with a friend. Think of six people, machines, other animals, or objects and say a **verb** to describe what they do!

Write a **verb** to describe something each animal might do!

11. kangaroo **hops** 14. butterfly **glides**
12. cheetah **runs** 15. monkey **swings**
13. penguin **waddles** 16. horse **gallops**

*Responses will vary.

42 Review: Nouns & Verbs

page 43

Review Section 3

Name: Date:

Review: Nouns & Verbs

Read each sentence. Circle each **noun**. Draw a box around the **main verbs**. Underline each **helping verb**.

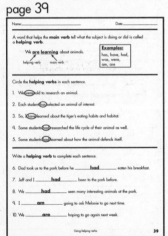

1. Yesterday, we were helping with yard work.
2. I was pulling weeds out of the flowerbeds.
3. Jackie and mom were planting flowers.
4. They had placed the dirt in the garden already.
5. The clouds grew dark, but it didn't rain.
6. We had fun helping each other!
7. The little girl was eating an enormous slice of pizza.
8. My grandma and I have baked delicious homemade brownies.
9. The sunset has made the evening quite romantic.
10. We have waited a long time for the movie to start!

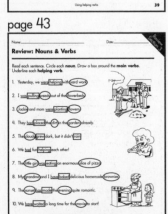

STOP! TAKE A BREAK! You did a great job! Place your Book Mark here & RELAX!

Review: Nouns & Verbs 43

page 44

Name: Date:

Subjects and **verbs** must agree. If the **subject** is singular (just one), the **verb** has to be singular. If the **subject** is plural (more than one), the **verb** has to be plural.

Read the sentences. Circle the correct **verb** to finish each sentence.

1. My friend and I (practice / practices) for the soccer match.
2. Jillian (know / knows) where to find the best pizza!
3. The farmers (ride / rides) huge tractors over the fields.
4. Those horses (gallop / gallops) on the muddy track.
5. A new family (live / lives) in that house on the corner.
6. We heard the scientists (speak / speaks) about the discovery.
7. Will that tiny ant really (move / moves) those crumbs?
8. Our teacher (grade / grades) our spelling tests right away.
9. I'd like to (jump / jumps) on the trampoline.
10. How did you (learn / learns) that poem so quickly?
11. She always (bake / bakes) muffins for breakfast.
12. Let's see if we can (take / takes) a walk later today.

Tip: Read the sentence out loud. If the verb sounds funny in the sentence, it's probably not the correct choice.

44 Subject-Verb Agreement

page 45

Name: Date:

Every sentence must have a **subject** and a **predicate**. The **subject** tells who or what is doing the action. The **predicate** tells what the subject does or is.

Tip: Remember – Every sentence begins with a capital letter and ends with a period.

The dogs bark.
subject predicate

Read each sentence. Draw one line under the **subject** and two lines under the **predicate**.

1. We organized a baseball game.
2. We played at the community park.
3. We won the game in an extra inning!
4. I thought the game would never be over.
5. Mom watched the game from the bleachers.
6. She cheered us on all afternoon!
7. The team had ice cream after the game.
8. I love ice cream as much as winning!

Identifying subjects and predicates 45

page 46

Name: Date:

Every sentence has two main parts.
1. **Subject** or the **naming part** tells who or what a sentence is about.
2. **Predicate** or the **action part** tells what a subject is or does.

Lions roar.
subject predicate

Read each sentence. Circle the **subject** and underline the **predicate**.

1. Our class went on a field trip to the zoo.
2. We bought our tickets and went in through the front gate.
3. The teacher divided our class up into small groups.
4. I was in the group with my two best friends.
5. We went to see the koalas first.
6. Emma wanted to see the elephants next.
7. Our group stopped at a park bench to have a snack while we watched the giraffes.
8. Jeanie and Lily wanted to see the cheetahs.
9. Mrs. Johnson said it was time to meet our class back at the front entrance.
10. We learned a whole lot about the different animals we saw that day.

46 Identifying subjects and predicates

Answers

page 47

Rewrite each group of words to make it a complete sentence with a **subject** and a **predicate**.

*Responses will vary

1. went to the store to buy flowers
Lena went to the store to buy flowers.
2. ben his mom if they could go to the store.
Ben asked his mom if they could go to the store.
3. Lauren and her brother in the yard
Lauren and her brother played in the yard.
4. is teaching her how to knit.
Grandma is teaching her how to knit.
5. grandpa early to go fishing.
Grandpa work up early to go fishing.

Write five complete sentences using the words in the box. Use each word or group of words once.

*Responses will vary

Gary and Michelle	Shelly and I	went to the library	took a boat to the island
Jonathan	We	played in the clubhouse	stood in line for an hour
The whole class		skated to my house	

6. **Gary and Michelle went to the library.**
7. **Jonathan played in the clubhouse.**
8. **Shelly and I skated to my house.**
9. **The whole class took a boat to the island.**
10. **We stood in line for an hour.**

Challenge: Find 5 newspaper headlines. If the headlines are not complete sentences, decide what is missing. Then, rewrite the headline to make it a complete sentence.

Writing complete sentences 47

page 48

Write a **subject** from the list (or make up your own) to complete each sentence.

They	Martin
The principal	The aquarium
The truck	The Smiths
We	Alexis and Karen
Grandma and grandpa	Ashley
The pet shop	Jack and Alan
Our class	The team

*Responses will vary.

1. **The principal** walked home from school today.
2. **Alexis and Karen** are on the same baseball team.
3. **We** earned an extra recess for excellent behavior.
4. **Grandma and grandpa** brought all the furniture to their new house.
5. **The pet shop** has practically every species of fish!
6. **The team** played outside all day.
7. **The Smiths** built a new clubhouse in their backyard.
8. **Martin** ordered a new red car.
9. **Ashley** thought they played their best game yet.
10. **Jack and Alan** watched a movie on Saturday afternoon.

48 Writing complete sentences

page 49

Write a **predicate** from the list (or make up your own) to complete each sentence.

went to the playground with her babysitter.
broke when my brother threw it on the floor.
planted a colorful bush in their garden.
was having a huge sale.
enjoyed the beautiful sunshine today.
was playing my favorite song.
is a healthy snack.
was very relaxing.
went to the pool for the day.

*Responses will vary.

1. They **went to the pool for the day.**
2. The toy **was broken.**
3. We **had fun at the parade.**
4. The radio **was playing my favorite song.**
5. My family **enjoyed the beautiful sunshine today.**
6. Jessica **planted a tree.**
7. An apple **is a healthy snack.**
8. The vacation **was very relaxing.**
9. The store **was having a huge sale.**
10. Their friends **went to the playground.**

Writing complete sentences 49

page 50

Read each sentence. Circle the **subject** and underline the **predicate**.

1. (Our family) goes on a vacation every year.
2. (The best vacation) was when we went to Washington, D.C.
3. (We) saw so many historic sites.
4. (My favorite part) was the tour of the White House.

*Responses will vary.

Write a **subject** to complete each sentence.

5. **Maxine** went to the library.
6. **Allie** and I ride bicycles together.
7. **Maryanne** was late getting to work yesterday.
8. **Double Dutch Dip** sells three flavors of ice cream.

Write a **predicate** to complete each sentence.

9. The man **ran out of chips.**
10. Jerry and Jason **love soccer.**
11. Natalie **wanted peanuts at the game.**
12. The boat **was red and blue.**

Tip: A predicate should have an action verb or a to be verb in it (i.e. is, am, are, was, were).

50 Writing complete sentences

page 51

Review: Editing Sentences

Rewrite each group of words to make complete and correct sentence with a **subject** and **predicate**.

1. the playground went to I
I went to the playground.
2. My aunt at the clothing store works
My aunt works at the clothing store.
3. monkey on the swing Do you see the
Do you see the monkey on the swing?
4. movie Lynn and I on Saturday saw a
Lynn and I saw a movie on Saturday.
5. two big dogs next live door
Two big dogs live next door.
6. My favorite checkers game is
My favorite game is checkers.
7. driving a red bird saw my father while to work
My father saw a red bird while driving to work.
8. got wet socks my
My socks got wet.
9. We decided to baseball play
We decided to play baseball.
10. home for a snack I came
I came home for a snack.

Review: Editing Sentences 51

page 52

Review: Editing Sentences

Rewrite the sentences with the correct punctuation, spelling, and grammar.

1. her new haircut is much shorter?
Her new haircut is much shorter.
2. I is so happy that it is mine birfday
I am so happy that it is my birthday!
3. It is n't time two go too the store yet
It isn't time to go to the store yet.
4. please hang up your clothes jacket and umbrella and put yer toy's away.
Please hang up your clothes, jacket, and umbrella and put your toys away.
5. Were were you yester day!
Where were you yesterday?
6. They bawght a new car that's red, green and wite.
They bought a new car that is red, green, and white.
7. When mom get hoMe i need to ask her a qestion?
When mom get's home, I need to ask her a question.
8. how long did it take he to makes that cake?
How long did it take her to make that cake?
9. This game was confusing because it does'nt has directions.
This game is confusing because it doesn't have directions.
10. do you's need anything from there store?
Do you need anything from the store?

52 Review: Editing Sentences

page 53

Review: Editing Sentences

Rewrite the sentence or sentences with the correct punctuation, spelling, and grammar.

1. I like too play baseball in the bulldogs team?
I like to play baseball on the Bulldogs team.
2. I goed to the feeld but th game, were cancelled, because of rane
I went to the field, but the game was cancelled because of rain.
3. john be sad becausehe want to try out her new baseball glove.
John was sad because he wanted to try out his new baseball glove.
4. When we leaved the field, Dad asked do we wanted to stop four icecream?
When we left the field, Dad asked if we wanted to stop for ice cream.
5. we got's to order a sundaes or a cones.
We got to order a sundae or a cone.
6. I ordering a duble scoop of chalkate and Dad ordering vanilla!
I ordered a double scoop of chocolate and Dad ordered vanilla!
7. We eight at a picnic table that, was, reelly. Long,
We ate at a picnic table that was really long.
8. It's was time to go so wee thanked dad!
It was time to go, so we thanked Dad!
9. On the way home, we talked about we talked about basket ball, and, baseball
On the way home, we talked about basketball and baseball.

You did a great job! Place your Book Mark here & RELAX!

Review: Editing Sentences 53

page 54

Make a list of five things that make you feel happy.

1.
2.
3. *Responses will vary.
4.
5.

Choose one of the things from your list and write a few sentences about it on the lines below. Be sure to explain why it makes you feel happy and give as many details as you can!

54 Writing notes, journals, and lists

page 55

Write a letter to a friend using the prompts below.

Date

Dear

*Responses will vary.

Did you ever wonder what you would do if you had a million dollars? Here's what I would do. First,

Then,

Finally,

Please write back soon and tell me what you would do!

Sincerely,

Writing a letter 55

page 56

Read the story and respond to the questions on the next page.

Sugar and Spice

Once a week, Michelle and Ryan stop by the pet shop on their way home from school. They stopped for two reasons—Sugar and Spice. Sugar and Spice are two kittens that shared a cage. They played so nicely together. Michelle and Ryan both had been begging their parents for a kitten. Since they are neighbors, they thought it would be perfect if Michelle got Sugar and Ryan got Spice.

Things got busy at school and home, so Michelle and Ryan didn't have time to stop by the pet shop. How they missed seeing Sugar and Spice! A few weeks later, Michelle and her mom passed by the pet shop. To Michelle's surprise, she didn't see Spice in the front window. She only saw Sugar. A terrible thought crossed her mind. Maybe someone bought Spice and the two best friends would never be together again. She went home practically in tears, but her mom assured her everything would be okay.

That weekend was Ryan's birthday party. Michelle was really looking forward to going because Ryan's parties were always fun. At the party they played games, sang, and ate cake and ice cream. Then came the best part—the presents! Ryan got lots of neat toys, including a few that Michelle was planning to put on her own birthday list. Just when Ryan thought he was done opening all the presents, his dad brought out a small box with holes in it and a bow on top. Ryan carefully opened the box and found Spice inside!

*See next page.

Ryan had mixed feelings. He was excited to have a new kitten, but he was also sad that Spice was not with his best friend Sugar anymore. Ryan's parents sensed his sad feeling and motioned for Michelle's mom. She stepped forward with a small box with holes in it and a bow on top. The box looked just like the one that Ryan got. Michelle's mom asked Michelle if she wanted an early birthday present. But before Michelle could answer, Ryan had the box open and Sugar was peeking out! Sugar and Spice immediately started playing together and Ryan looked at Michelle and said, "This is the best birthday ever!"

56 Writing a response to text

page 57

Think about the story *Sugar and Spice* from the previous page. Write your personal responses to the questions below. Use complete sentences.

1. Do you think Sugar and Spice will continue to be best friends? Why or why not?
2. What was your favorite part in the story? Describe it.
3. Explain how you think they felt when they saw Sugar and Spice together again.

*Responses will vary.

4. Describe how you think Ryan's feelings changed after Michelle opened her early birthday present.
5. Who do you think is happier, Ryan and Michelle or Sugar and Spice? Why?
6. How would you feel if you received a gift like Sugar and Spice?
7. If you could get a special pet of your own, what kind of animal would you like and why?

Writing a response to text 57

page 58

Think about an exciting time that you shared with a family member, such as going camping with Grandpa, going to a concert with Mom, or visiting an amusement park with your cousin. Write your special moment on the line.

My exciting moment is:

Write some details about your exciting moment in the box.

*Responses will vary.

Tip: Try to create pictures in your mind of what you saw, smelled, touched, heard, tasted, or how you felt. Then, use words to help recreate that for the reader!

Write a paragraph (or several sentences) about your exciting moment using the supporting details that you wrote in the box.

58 Writing a descriptive paragraph or simple story

page 59

Review: Writing

Write a **noun, verb,** or **compound word** on each blank space to create your own story! Look below each line so you know what kind of word to write. Then, read your story.

Last Halloween, I decided to dress up as a ______ (noun). My best friend, ______ (proper noun/name), dressed as a ______ (noun). The evening was cold and dark. We ______ (verb) and ______ (verb) down the street until we came to the ______ (noun) on the corner. The ______ (plural noun) was piled high around the front door and no lights were on. Suddenly, we heard a sound coming from the ______ (compound word). We almost ______ (verb) right on the spot!

*Responses will vary.

Luckily, my friend had a flashlight! We aimed it at the ______ (compound word) and ______ (verb) when we realized it was only a ______ (noun). I couldn't believe it! We were so relieved that we ______ (verb). Once we had our fill of ______ (noun), we ______ (verb) back home. Our treat bags were loaded with ______ (plural noun). I can hardly wait for Halloween next year!

Review: Writing 59

page 60

Review: Writing

Think about your favorite animal and what might happen if that animal lived with you. Write a short story about this silly idea.

Title:

Beginning:

Tip: Capitalize the first letters in your title. Be sure to use complete sentences in your story!

*Responses will vary.

Middle:

End:

You did a great job! Place your Book Mark here & RELAX!

60 Review: Writing

20 QUESTIONS? JEOPARDY-STYLE!

1. Take the game board with you anywhere and see how quickly you can answer the items in order from 1 to 20. Play alone or challenge a friend!
2. When you answer each question, you must phrase your answer in the form of a question.

Example for #1 -
What are...a hot dog, a hula-hoop, and a bikini?

---

1. Identify 3 *nouns* to describe what you might see at the beach.

2. Name 3 *verbs* to describe what people might do at the mall.

3. Name 4 things that a complete sentence must include.

4. Tell & spell the *plural* of these nouns: party, child, car, fox & dish

6. Identify 2 words that have this *suffix:* -est

5. Identify 2 words that have this *prefix:* poly-

7. Tell 1 example of when you might use an *apostrophe.*

8. Tell the *abbreviation* for your birth month, your state & the day of the week.

9. Tell 5 of your favorite foods. Say *"comma"* to show where each comma belongs between your foods.

10. Say a word or phrase that could end with an *exclamation mark!*

13. Identify 4 words that begin with a *capital letter.*

12. Use these words in a *complete sentence:* phone, car, eat.

11. Give an example of a *question.*

14. Name 3 places that are *common nouns.*

15. Give 5 examples of *proper nouns.*

16. Use the *past tense* of 3 verbs to tell what you did yesterday.

17. Say 3 unique facts about you - use the correct form of the verb *to be.*

18. Identify 3 important parts of a *friendly letter.*

20. Say an example of a complete sentence. Identify the *subject & predicate.*

19. Identify the 3 *main parts* of your favorite fairy tale.

©2009 Learning Horizons, Inc.

SKILL CHECKLIST!

_____'s

YOUR NAME

WOO HOO!

Use this Skill Checklist to check off the skills as you practice them in the book.

- ☐ Root Words & Compound Words
- ☐ Prefixes & Suffixes
- ☐ Contractions & Abbreviations
- ☐ Punctuation: " ' , .!?"
- ☐ Spelling Words
- ☐ Nouns & Verbs
- ☐ Writing Complete Sentences
- ☐ Informal Writing – lists, notes, etc.
- ☐ Writing Letters & Responses
- ☐ Writing Stories

COMPOUND WORD BRAINSTORM

1. Take the game board with you anywhere & have fun with compound words!
2. Choose a word from the list & try to identify as many compound words as possible.
   (i.e. sea – seashell, sea shore, seasick, seascape)
3. Take turns with a friend until you run out of ideas, then move to another word.
4. Find compound words as you travel!
   (i.e. highway? inlet? underpass? ladybug?)

news	flower	pig	hand
blue	lady	finger	eye
bed	air	back	head
day	down	ear	foot
grand	high	in	life
night	out	over	under
heart	egg	good	pin

HEARD ANY JOKES LATELY?

1. Take this noun game and play while you wait, on the road, or anywhere!
2. Roll a die, or just choose a number between 1 & 6 for the joke-starters below.
3. Choose a noun, verb or plural noun to fill the blanks in that joke-starter.
4. Then, see who can create the silliest answer! Be creative!

1. What do you call a _____ with a _____ ?
   noun   noun

2. How many _____ does it take to _____ ?
   plural noun   verb

3. Why did the _____ cross the road?
   noun

4. What did the _____ say to the _____ ?
   noun   noun

5. What is a _____'s favorite _____ ?
   noun   noun

6. What do you get when you cross a _____ and a _____ ?
   noun   noun

Example: Why did the bunny cross the road?
To get to her "hare" (hair) appointment!